Vision Beyond Dreams

An insightful effects of Apple Vision
pro's innovative technologies.

Richard joe

Table of Contents

Introduction

In the ever-evolving landscape of technology, the profound impact it has on our lives cannot be overstated. This essay will delve into the intricate tapestry of technological evolution, exploring its roots, trajectory, and the transformative power it wields. By unraveling the layers that constitute the essence of technology, we aim to shed light on its significance in shaping the world we inhabit.

Unveiling the Vision: Setting the Stage

To comprehend the essence of technology, one must first grasp the vision that propels its advancement.

The inception of technology is often rooted in the human desire for progress, efficiency, and innovation. From the earliest tools crafted by our ancestors to the sophisticated systems of today, a common thread binds them – the aspiration to improve the human experience. The vision behind technology is multifaceted, encompassing a spectrum of motives. It could be the pursuit of convenience, the quest for knowledge, or the ambition to overcome challenges. As societies progressed, so did the scope of technological vision. The Industrial Revolution, for instance, marked a pivotal moment where the vision expanded to encompass mass production and the mechanization of labor.

In contemporary times, the vision extends into realms like artificial intelligence, sustainable development, and connectivity. The stage is set for a future where technology not only addresses immediate needs but also anticipates and adapts to the changing dynamics of our global society. Unveiling this vision requires a nuanced understanding of the interplay between human aspirations and technological innovation.

Evolution of Technology: A Brief Overview

The journey of technology unfolds through epochs, each characterized by breakthroughs that redefine the boundaries of human capability.

The primitive tools of ancient civilizations, such as the wheel and simple agricultural implements, marked the embryonic stages of technological evolution. These innovations were driven by the need for survival and the improvement of daily life. The Middle Ages witnessed incremental advancements, with innovations like the printing press and navigation tools shaping the contours of society. However, it was the Renaissance that ushered in a new era of transformative technology, fostering a climate conducive to exploration and discovery. The scientific revolution further accelerated progress, laying the groundwork for the industrialization that would follow.

The 19th and 20th centuries witnessed a cascade of technological marvels – from the steam engine to electricity, telecommunication to space exploration. Each innovation built upon its predecessor, creating a tapestry of progress that spans continents and centuries. The digital age, a recent chapter in this saga, has revolutionized communication, information access, and the very fabric of daily life. The evolution of technology is not a linear trajectory but a complex interplay of societal needs, scientific discovery, and inventive minds. It reflects a continuous cycle of problem-solving and adaptation. As technology evolves, it not only addresses existing challenges but also paves the way for new possibilities, sometimes reshaping the very questions we ask.

Understanding the motivations driving technological innovation and tracing its historical path provides a foundation for analyzing its current state and envisioning the possibilities that lie ahead. The journey through the landscape of technology promises insights into the dynamic relationship between human ingenuity and the tools that define our progress.

Chapter 1:The Genesis of Apple Vision Pro

Few companies have had such a dramatic impact on the ever-changing technological world as Apple. This chapter delves deeply into the origins of one of Apple's most breakthrough products, the Apple Vision Pro. From its inception to the main visionaries piloting the ship, we uncover the story of this remarkable product's progress.

Origins & Development

The origins of Apple Vision Pro may be traced back to the company's unwavering commitment to innovation.

As the internet behemoth tried to push the frontiers of user experience, the concept of combining cutting-edge technology with immersive visual experiences emerged. The idea was to build a seamless combination of augmented reality (AR) and intuitive features, which paved the way for the creation of Apple Vision Pro. The development period saw painstaking planning, research, and engineering expertise. Apple's dedication to perfection was reflected in the use of high-quality materials, ergonomic design, and a user-centric approach.

The road from idea to prototype included overcoming several hurdles, ranging from hardware complexities to software optimization, ending in a product that intended not just to meet but surpass consumer expectations. Apple's iterative design process included feedback loops and revisions. The user experience was prioritized, ensuring that the Apple Vision Pro will smoothly fit into consumers' life, serving as not just a gadget but also an unprecedented portal to a new digital environment. The product's progress reflected the rigorous attention to detail and devotion to innovation that have come to define the Apple brand.

Key Visionaries Behind Innovation

Behind every remarkable invention, there are visionaries who set the route and mold the future. The creation of Apple Vision Pro is no exception, with prominent players playing critical roles in its conception and execution. Steve Jobs, Apple's visionary co-founder, established the basis for an innovative culture that still thrives today. His insight and drive for pushing technical frontiers paved the way for initiatives like the Apple Vision Pro. While Jobs was not directly engaged in its creation, his impact is felt across the organization, motivating a dedication to quality and user-centric design.

Tim Cook: As the torchbearer of Apple's history, Tim Cook took on the job of CEO, focusing on preserving innovation and growing Apple's influence. Under his guidance, the Apple Vision Pro project gained traction, thanks to Cook's strategic vision and devotion to putting Apple at the forefront of technical breakthroughs. Jony Ive, renowned as Apple's design genius, was instrumental in developing the hardware and aesthetics of the Apple Vision Pro. His design philosophy, which emphasizes simplicity, beauty, and utility, is visible in every curve and shape of the gadget.

Ive's influence went beyond the surface and into the product's core, providing a seamless marriage of form and function. These important visionaries, along with a devoted team of engineers, designers, and inventors, gave rise to the Apple Vision Pro. Their joint efforts turned an idea into a physical reality, highlighting Apple's long history of pioneering achievements.

Chapter 2:Technological Marvels

In terms of technical innovation, Apple Vision Pro is a monument to the quest of greatness. This chapter goes into the device's complexities, uncovering its cutting-edge capabilities and analyzing the developments in image and sensing technologies that raise it to the position of a technical wonder.

An in-depth look at Apple Vision Pro's cutting-edge features

The Apple Vision Pro is more than just a gadget; it's a synthesis of cutting-edge technology precisely designed to transform user experiences.

At its heart, the smartphone has a slew of cutting-edge capabilities that all add to its attraction. Integration with Augmented Reality (AR): The seamless integration of augmented reality is the pinnacle of Apple Vision Pro's capabilities. The technology breaks down conventional barriers by superimposing digital information on the actual environment in real time. Whether it's traversing a city with interactive overlays or playing immersive AR games, AR integration boosts user engagement and changes the way people interact with their environment.

Ultra-responsive Haptic Feedback: Apple Vision Pro's ultra-responsive haptic technology adds a new layer to user feedback. Users may not only see and hear interactions, but also feel them, providing a tactile element to the digital experience. This subtle haptic input improves the device's usefulness by making interactions more intuitive and immersive.

Immersive Display Technology: The gadget has cutting-edge display technology that captivates the senses. An immersive visual experience is achieved by high resolution, rich colors, and strong contrasts. The display acts as a doorway to a visually attractive digital environment, whether you're viewing movies, surfing material, or using AR apps.

Intelligent speech Recognition: Apple Vision Pro uses powerful speech recognition technology that goes beyond basic instructions. The gadget recognizes context, learns user preferences, and adjusts to individual speech patterns. This intuitive speech interface makes it easier for users to operate and communicate with the gadget.

Biometric Security protections: Security is critical, and Apple Vision Pro puts it first with advanced biometric protections. Facial recognition technology, along with modern sensors, guarantees safe user identification. This seamless integration of security elements both protects user data and improves the overall user experience.

Innovations in Imaging and Sensing Technologies

Apple Vision Pro's technical strength goes beyond surface-level features to include the advanced image and sensor technologies that support its performance.

Depth-sensing Cameras: The gadget has powerful depth-sensing cameras for accurate spatial mapping. This technology is essential to the AR experience because it enables the device to precisely interpret its surroundings and overlay digital content. The depth-sensing capabilities also contribute to sophisticated photographic features, resulting in spectacular photographs with improved depth perception.

LiDAR Technology: Light Detection and Ranging (LiDAR) technology transforms the sensing capabilities of Apple Vision Pro. This laser-based device allows for quick and precise distance measurements, which improves AR applications and adds to immersive experiences. LiDAR enhances the device's functioning in a variety of ways, including accurate item positioning and enhanced low-light photography.

Smart Sensors for Environmental Awareness: Apple Vision Pro includes a variety of smart sensors that improve environmental awareness. These sensors monitor ambient light, temperature, and motion, enabling the gadget to autonomously adapt to its environment.

These sensors add to a dynamic and responsive user experience by altering display brightness in response to ambient light or improving performance depending on user activities.

Advanced Machine Learning Integration: The gadget continually improves its capabilities using machine learning techniques. Machine learning guarantees that Apple Vision Pro grows and adapts to the demands of users over time, from improving face recognition accuracy to optimizing speech recognition depending on user behavior.

Chapter 3:The Insightful Effect

In the continuation of technical innovation, the influence of a new item goes beyond specs and functionalities. Chapter 3 delves into the Apple Vision Pro's tremendous influence on daily life and the dramatic advances it brings to numerous sectors. This chapter explores the revolutionary impact of this innovative instrument, ranging from changing everyday experiences to transforming whole industries.

Understanding the Impact in Everyday Life

The Apple Vision Pro is more than simply a gadget; it is a catalyst for new possibilities that blend into the fabric of everyday life. This section investigates the device's influence on numerous aspects of daily living, providing insight into how it alters routines, interactions, and experiences.

Increased Productivity and Connectivity: One of the most significant benefits of Apple Vision Pro is its contribution to increased productivity. With its augmented reality capabilities, users may effortlessly overlay digital information on their actual surroundings, redefining how activities are performed. From interactive virtual meetings to collaborative workplaces, the gadget pushes the frontiers of remote work and ushers in a new age of connectedness.

Immersive Entertainment and Gaming:
The device's advanced display technology and augmented reality capabilities transform entertainment and gaming experiences. Users may immerse themselves in interactive storytelling, explore virtual worlds, and play augmented reality games. The line between reality and digital material is becoming more blurred, providing previously inconceivable levels of immersion.

Transformational Educational Experiences: In the field of education, the Apple Vision Pro serves as a catalyst for transformational learning experiences. Augmented reality apps bring history to life, allow for interactive scientific investigations, and provide immersive language learning settings.

The gadget goes beyond standard instructional tools, becoming a dynamic platform that promotes inquiry and involvement.

Seamless Navigation and Exploration: The device functions as a customized navigator, providing real-time information and direction. From navigating city streets with AR overlays to discovering new places with interactive guides, Apple Vision Pro transforms how people engage with and perceive their environment. The seamless integration of location-based information improves both navigation and the overall exploring experience.

Health and wellbeing Integration: Apple Vision Pro has new features that promote health and wellbeing. From augmented reality exercises to real-time health monitoring, the gadget becomes a trusted friend on customers' travels to a healthy living. The enlightening effect extends to encouraging well-being, with technology assisting users in their quest of physical and mental health.

Revolutionary Changes in Various Industries

The effect of Apple Vision Pro extends beyond individual experiences, infiltrating numerous sectors and spurring revolutionary change. This section investigates the device's transformational impact across industries, which challenges established procedures and raises industry standards.

Healthcare and Medical Applications:
Apple Vision Pro is poised to revolutionize the healthcare industry. Surgeons may use augmented reality to perform precise procedures and see important information in real time. Patients benefit from augmented reality therapy and individualized health monitoring. The gadget promotes a paradigm change in healthcare delivery by improving diagnosis, treatment, and patient participation.

Retail & Shopping Experiences: Apple Vision Pro revolutionizes the retail scene. Augmented reality changes the way people buy by enabling them to virtually try on things before purchasing. Retailers use AR to provide interactive in-store displays and tailored suggestions.

The gadget serves as a bridge between the physical and digital worlds, improving the overall purchasing experience.

Architecture and Design Integration: The Apple Vision Pro allows architects and designers to explore new creative possibilities. The gadget enables immersive 3D modeling and visualization, enabling experts to walk around virtual versions of their creations. This transforms the design process by encouraging cooperation and improving the transmission of complicated ideas to customers.

Manufacturing and Maintenance Enhancements: Apple Vision Pro helps simplify production operations and maintenance routines. AR-guided workflows increase production floor productivity, and workers use augmented reality to maintain and repair equipment. The gadget becomes an essential tool for improving operational accuracy and decreasing downtimes.

Tourist and hotel Transformation: The Apple Vision Pro creates a transformational change in the tourist and hotel sector. Visitors may visit historical places using interactive AR guides, while hotels provide augmented reality concierge services. The gadget enhances travel experiences by offering a seamless combination of information and entertainment to travelers.

Chapter 4:User Experience and Integration

In the world of technology, user experience (UX) and integration are critical variables in determining a product's success and resonance. Chapter 4 goes into the complexities of the Apple Vision Pro, examining how its user experience is precisely designed to deliver a smooth interaction path. We also look at its integration into the larger Apple ecosystem, exploring how the iPad works with other Apple devices to provide a unified and immersive user experience.

Navigate the User Interface

The Apple Vision Pro's user interface (UI) serves as a doorway to its many capabilities, which have been meticulously crafted to provide an intuitive and immersive experience. This section delves deeply into the UI aspects, studying how users browse and interact with the device.

Intuitive Gestures and Controls: Apple Vision Pro includes a set of intuitive gestures and controls that transform user interactions. From basic swipes and taps to more complex hand gestures, the device reacts effortlessly, resulting in a natural and fluid user experience. These motions are not only utilitarian, but also deliberately crafted to increase the overall sensation of participation and control.

Configurable Interface: Recognizing the wide range of user preferences, the device provides a configurable interface that conforms to individual requirements. Users may customize the layout, prioritize commonly used functions, and change the overall appearance and feel of the UI. This focus on personalization allows users to shape the gadget according to their own tastes, instilling a feeling of ownership and familiarity.

Augmented Reality Navigation: The user interface is tightly linked to the device's augmented reality capabilities. Users may easily browse among apps, messages, and information overlays in their actual surroundings. Augmented reality goes beyond a visual spectacle; it becomes an intrinsic element of the navigational experience, seamlessly blending the digital and physical worlds together.

Speech-guided Interactions: The Apple Vision Pro utilizes powerful speech recognition technology to provide voice-guided interactions. Users may operate the gadget, retrieve information, and execute orders using natural and conversational speech. This hands-free technique improves accessibility while also adding a degree of convenience to the user experience.

Seamless Integration with the Apple Ecosystem

Apple's dedication to a smooth and integrated user experience is shown by the Apple Vision Pro's seamless connection with the larger Apple ecosystem.

This section investigates how the gadget interacts with other Apple goods, resulting in a unified ecosystem that improves the overall user experience.

Continuity Across Devices: The Apple Vision Pro interacts effortlessly with other Apple devices, offering a consistent user experience. Users may begin a job on their iPhone, continue it on their MacBook, then seamlessly switch to the Apple Vision Pro. This continuity boosts productivity and ensures a consistent user experience across the ecosystem.

Handoff features enable users to smoothly move work across devices. Whether drafting an email, surfing material, or participating in an AR experience, users may easily transfer activities from their iPhone or iPad to the Apple Vision Pro and vice versa. This function avoids disturbances and improves the flow of user interactions.

Universal Accessibility Features: The Apple ecosystem's dedication to universal accessibility extends to the Apple Vision Pro. VoiceOver, Magnifier, and Sound Recognition are common features on Apple devices that smoothly blend into the device's functioning. This guarantees a uniform and inclusive user experience for a wide variety of users with different requirements.

Synced Data and apps: The synchronization of data and apps across Apple devices is a key feature of the ecosystem integration. The Apple Vision Pro provides smooth access to synchronized information, ensuring that contacts, calendars, and programs are up to date. This coordinated environment streamlines the user's digital experience, generating a feeling of cohesiveness and efficiency.

Cross-device Communication: The Apple Vision Pro enables cross-device communication across the ecosystem. Users may easily accept phone calls, react to messages, and get alerts regardless of whatever Apple device they are using. This interconnectivity increases convenience by enabling customers to remain connected and informed across several Apple devices.

Chapter 5:Challenges and Innovations

How to Overcome Obstacles in Pursuing Visionary Goals

Pursuing ambitious objectives is a difficult road, but overcoming these difficulties is where great creativity arises. This section explores the perilous terrain where dreams and obstacles collide, presenting tales of perseverance and persistence.

Technological Obstacles: Technological challenges loom big when developing breakthrough gadgets such as the Apple Vision Pro. The creation of cutting-edge features and developments need answers to complex difficulties, ranging from providing flawless augmented reality experiences to overcoming hardware restrictions. Innovators confront the daunting job of pushing the limits of what is possible, and each accomplishment demonstrates their capacity to overcome technical difficulties.

Market Dynamics and Competition: Navigating dynamics and competition in a quickly changing market is an ongoing task. Pioneering items often challenge established conventions, prompting scrutiny and rivalry. Overcoming established players' opposition and carving out a niche needs strategic thinking and adaptation. The chapter delves into how visionary aspirations endure in the face of market obstacles, creating a story of resilience and market innovation.

Regulatory and Ethical concerns: There are several regulatory and ethical concerns that must be addressed while developing and deploying innovative technology. Maintaining compliance with standards, navigating legal frameworks, and resolving ethical problems requires a fine balance. Overcoming these challenges requires a commitment to responsible innovation, in which innovators aim for both technical brilliance and ethical integrity.

User Adoption and Acceptance: The achievement of visionary objectives is inextricably linked to user adoption and acceptance. Convincing consumers to adopt new technology, particularly ones that transform their everyday lives, is a huge problem.

Addressing user issues, ensuring smooth integration into everyday life, and building trust become critical. This section describes the path of overcoming opposition and gaining hearts, demonstrating the symbiotic link between innovation and user acceptability.

Continuous Innovation and Future Prospects

Innovation is not a static accomplishment, but rather a dynamic process that drives continual progress. This section of Chapter 5 tells the story of continuous innovation, examining how overcoming obstacles serves as a catalyst for continued progress and defines the future possibilities of creative efforts.

Iterative Development Cycles: Iterative development cycles describe the process of overcoming obstacles in order to achieve visionary objectives. Each challenge provides a chance for refinement and improvement. Innovators use a continuous feedback loop to learn from failures and iteratively improve their products. This iterative method becomes a pillar in the ongoing quest of excellence.

Collaborative Ecosystems: The innovation environment is moving in favor of collaborative ecosystems. Visionary objectives are increasingly being realized via multidisciplinary cooperation, in which varied expertise comes together to tackle problems.

This collaborative culture not only speeds invention, but also helps to create comprehensive solutions that solve several challenges.

Artificial Intelligence Symbiosis: Artificial intelligence (AI) develops as a transformational force, augmenting the capabilities of forward-thinking technology.

The confluence of human inventiveness with AI-driven improvements becomes a driving force in ongoing progress. This section explains how AI helps to overcome obstacles and advance ambitious aims into unexplored territory.

Sustainability and ethical innovation: The future possibilities of visionary projects are inextricably linked to environmental and ethical issues. Innovators are increasingly recognizing the necessity of developing technologies that not only push the envelope but do so ethically. This chapter investigates how sustainability and ethical innovation influence the trajectory of continual breakthroughs, assuring a future in which technology is aligned with social ideals.

Anticipating User demands: Continuous innovation goes beyond solving existing difficulties to anticipate future user demands.

Visionaries try to design technologies that fulfill current needs while also adapting to changing expectations. The story develops as innovators dig into user-centric design, keeping ahead of the curve and designing a future in which technology blends effortlessly into the fabric of everyday life.

Chapter 6:Beyond Dreams

Envisioning Future Possibilities

The future is a blank canvas ready to be painted with the brushstrokes of creativity and ingenuity. This part digs into the possibilities that lie ahead, investigating various technology landscapes and social shifts that may arise.

AI and Enhanced Intelligence Augmentation: As we look forward, the relationship between artificial intelligence (AI) and human capacities becomes more important. The Apple Vision Pro, which is already a forerunner of augmented reality experiences, might develop into a platform that connects easily with sophisticated AI systems.

This partnership might usher in a new age of enhanced intelligence augmentation, in which people are empowered by AI-driven insights and capabilities that go beyond present limitations.

Immersive Extended Reality (XR) Experiences: The growth of augmented reality (AR) and virtual reality (VR) is set to reshape our perception and interaction with the digital and physical worlds. Imagine a future in which the Apple Vision Pro serves as a doorway to immersive extended reality experiences, blurring the gap between virtual and real. From realistic virtual travel experiences to interactive instructional simulations, the possibilities are limitless.

Sustainable and Eco-conscious Innovations: The future necessitates a greater emphasis on sustainability and environmentally responsible technology. The Apple Vision Pro may develop to include capabilities that promote a more sustainable future. Consider gadgets made with eco-friendly materials, energy-efficient components, and apps that raise environmental consciousness. The use of technology in promoting sustainability becomes a critical component of future possibilities.

Health and Wellness Revolution: The convergence of technology and healthcare is set to intensify, with the Apple Vision Pro leading the way. Future generations might feature enhanced health monitoring, individualized wellness programs, and real-time diagnoses. The gadget has the potential to become a proactive health companion, helping to usher in a new era of preventative healthcare and wellness.

Humanitarian and Global connection projects: Imagine a world in which technology, including the Apple Vision Pro, serves as a catalyst for global connection and humanitarian projects. From providing remote medical consultations in underprivileged areas to enabling immersive cultural encounters, the technology has the potential to bridge divides and build a feeling of global connection.

Apple Vision Pro's Contribution to Shaping Tomorrow

As we investigate future possibilities, the Apple Vision Pro emerges as a crucial actor, with the ability to change tomorrow's technological world. This section digs into the device's critical role in shaping the course of innovation and social changes.

Continued improvements and Iterations:
The Apple Vision Pro, renowned for its
dedication to quality, is set to experience more
improvements and iterations. Future versions
may have more powerful processors, advanced
sensors, and better design aesthetics. The
device's growth will most likely be marked by a
continuous quest of excellence and an
uncompromising dedication to satisfying the
changing demands of customers.

Integration with new Technologies: The
future promises the convergence of numerous
new technologies, and the Apple Vision Pro is
anticipated to lead this integration. From
seamless connection with Internet of Things
(IoT) devices to synergies with blockchain for
increased security, the device has the potential

to become a major hub within a larger ecosystem of linked technologies.

Augmenting Human Potential: As AI and augmented reality technologies evolve, the Apple Vision Pro's role in enhancing human potential becomes more important. Beyond being a source of information and entertainment, it has the potential to become a tool for improving cognitive capacities, creativity, and productivity. The gadget might become a buddy, allowing users to discover new aspects of their own potential.

Shaping society Norms and Expectations: Technological advances have a significant influence on society norms, and the Apple Vision Pro is well positioned to mold these standards.

Future incarnations might impact how we interact, work, learn, and experience reality. The technology might influence expectations about privacy, connection, and the balance between the digital and physical worlds.

Empowering Diverse sectors: The Apple Vision Pro's effect goes beyond personal usage to a variety of sectors. The device's capabilities have the potential to redefine the way education and healthcare, as well as industry and entertainment, work. The story of its role in molding future is on helping sectors to accept new opportunities and creative ways.

Conclusion

This investigation, similar to a technical adventure, takes us through the diverse development of the Apple Vision Pro. From its origin to the presentation of cutting-edge features and the expectation of future possibilities, each chapter tells a story of invention, obstacles, and the unwavering pursuit of ambitious aims.

Reflections on the Journey

The excursion demonstrates the iterative nature of technological advancement. The Apple concept Pro began as a concept and evolved into a technical wonder via iterative development cycles, overcoming challenges and creating an immersive user experience. The chapters tell a tale of persistence, flexibility, and a dedication to user-centered design. As we ponder, the journey becomes a dynamic interaction between visionary thought and the transformational force of making ideas a reality. In examining the technical wonders, obstacles, and ongoing advances around the Apple Vision Pro, the tale illustrates a connection between human inventiveness and the changing technological scene. It is more than just a technology; it is a symbol of progress and a force for molding the future.

Implications for the Future

The consequences of this voyage go well beyond the scope of a single gadget. The Apple Vision Pro sets a standard for future expectations, determining the course of technological growth. Its transformational influence in cultural standards, ethical issues, and global connectedness shows the device's greater significance. As we look forward, ethical questions become more important. The ramifications include not simply technological breakthroughs, but also a greater understanding of responsible innovation.

The Apple Vision Pro's involvement in global networking and humanitarian activities foreshadows a future in which technology becomes a force for good, encouraging cooperation and bridging divides.

Furthermore, individual empowerment takes center stage as the technology promotes personal progress and potential realization. The Apple Vision Pro may one day become a symbol of how technology can unleash individual creativity, productivity, and well-being.

www.ingramcontent.com/pod-product-compliance
Lightning Source LLC
LaVergne TN
LVHW051619050326
832903LV00033B/4573